HOUGHTON MIFFLIN

Georgia Science

HOUGHTON MIFFLIN

Printed in the U.S.A.
ISBN 13: 978-0-547-12511-4
ISBN 10: 0-547-12511-9

13 14 15 0928 19 18 17 16

4500590699

Contents

Weather and Seasons

 KWL

What Do You Know?

Talk with a partner.

Tell about today's weather.

Tell about yesterday's weather.

_____

_____

_____

Contents

What Do You Want to Know?

What else do you wonder about weather?

_____

_____

3

VOCABULARY

weather What the air outside is like. *(noun)*

VOCABULARY ACTIVITY

Classify Words

weather

Weather is what the air outside is like. What kinds of weather do you know?

_____

_____

S1E1a. Identify different types of weather and the characteristics of each type.

1 What Is Weather?

Weather is what the air outside is like.

There are many kinds of weather.

Weather may be warm or cool.

Weather may be sunny or cloudy.

warm and sunny

Weather may be windy.

Weather may be rainy, too.

You can see and feel weather.

windy

rainy

1. Draw an X on the picture of a windy day.

2. Draw a rainy day.

CRCT Prep

Circle the correct answer.

3. **Which word describes the weather shown?**

   (A) sunny

   (B) windy

   (C) rainy

S1E1a

5

I Wonder . . . Weather changes from day to day. At noon it is warm and sunny. Later it begins to rain. How did the sky change?

_____

_____

_____

Ways Weather Changes

Monday	cloudy	
Tuesday	rainy	
Wednesday	sunny	

Weather Changes

Weather can change
from day to day.
One day may be sunny
and warm.
The next day may be cloudy
and cool.
Then clouds may bring rain.

Main Idea

What are some kinds
of weather?

Summary   Weather is what the air outside is like. Tell about weather you know.

_____

_____

▶ **Main Idea**   What are some kinds of weather?

```
   ⬭      ⬭      ⬭
        |  |  |
   ⎯⎯⎯⎯⎯⎯⎯⎯⎯⎯⎯⎯
   Main Idea
   Weather changes from
   day to day
   ⎯⎯⎯⎯⎯⎯⎯⎯⎯⎯⎯⎯
      |        |
    ⬭          ⬭
```

7

VOCABULARY

temperature How warm or cool something is. *(noun)*

thermometer A tool that measures temperature. *(noun)*

VOCABULARY ACTIVITY

Use Words

temperature

Circle words on the pages that tell about temperature.

 S1E1b. Investigate weather by observing, measuring with simple weather instruments (thermometer, wind vane, rain gauge), and recording weather data (temperature, precipitation, sky conditions, and weather events) in a periodic journal or on a calendar seasonally.

8

2 How Can You Measure Weather?

You can use tools to tell about weather.

A **thermometer** is a tool that measures temperature.

Temperature is how warm or cool something is.

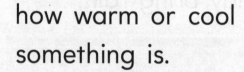

You can tell what to wear
by the temperature.
You wear warm clothes
when it is cold.
You wear clothes that keep you
cool when it is hot.

°F   °C

1. Circle the thermometer that
shows that the weather
temperature is hot.

2. Draw clothes that people would
wear in warm and cold weather.

a. warm

b. cold

3. What tool measures wind speed?

_____

Draw it.

4. What tools shows which way the wind blows?

_____

Draw it.

Tools for Wind and Rain

You can use tools
to measure the wind.
A windsock and a wind vane
show which way the wind blows.
A windsock shows
how hard the wind blows.

windsock

wind vane

You can use a tool
to measure rain.
A rain gauge measures
how much rain falls.

rain gauge

Draw Conclusions

What can you tell
about the wind if a windsock
is hanging down?

Summary You can use tools to
measure weather. Draw the tools
that measure weather.

▶ **Draw Conclusions** What can
you tell about the wind when a
windsock is hanging down?

Fact: A windsock shows how hard
the wind is blowing.

Fact: A windsock is hanging down.

Conclusion:

11

VOCABULARY

water cycle Water moving from Earth to the sky and back again. *(noun)*

cloud Many drops of water together. *(noun)*

VOCABULARY ACTIVITY

Use Pictures

water cycle

Look at the picture. Use your finger to trace the way that water moves back and forth to Earth.

S1E2b. Identify forms of precipitation such as rain, snow, sleet, and hailstone as either solid (ice) or liquid (water).

3 What Are Clouds and Rain?

Water moves from place to place.

A **water cycle** is when water moves from Earth to the sky and back again.

1 The Sun warms water. Some warm water goes into the air. You cannot see it.

2 Water in the air cools. Tiny drops of water make up a **cloud**.

3 Some drops get bigger. The drops fall back to Earth as rain.

1. How does water fall to Earth?

_____

2. Draw the water cycle.

GPS CRCT Prep

Circle the correct answer.

3. Which word tells one way that water returns to Earth?

  Ⓐ rain

  Ⓑ river

  Ⓒ ocean

S1E2b

13

4. Point to each cloud and say its name.

Draw each cloud.

Cumulus

Cirrus

Stratus

Kinds of Clouds

There are many kinds of clouds.
Clouds have different shapes.
Clouds have different colors.
Look at clouds to see
how weather changes.
These clouds are thin.
It may rain in a day or two.

cirrus clouds

Some clouds are puffy and white.
They can turn gray and
bring rain.
Some clouds are low and gray.
They may bring rain or snow.

cumulus clouds

stratus clouds

Cause and Effect

What can clouds tell you
about changes in the weather?

Summary   Water moving from
Earth to the sky and back again is
called the water cycle.

What happens when tiny drops of
water in clouds get bigger?

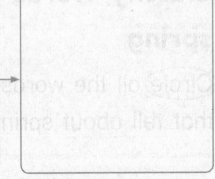 **Cause and Effect**   What can
clouds tell you about changes in
the weather?

Cause	Effect
You see gray clouds low in the sky.	

VOCABULARY

season A time of year that has its own kind of weather. *(noun)*

spring The season that follows winter. *(noun)*

summer The season that follows spring. *(noun)*

VOCABULARY ACTIVITY

Classify Words

spring

Circle all the words on these pages that tell about spring.

16   **S1E1c.** Correlate weather data (temperature, precipitation, sky conditions, and weather events) to seasonal changes.

4 What Is Weather Like in Spring and Summer?

A **season** is a time of year. It has its own kind of weather.

Spring

Spring is the season that follows winter. It is warmer in spring. Warmer weather and spring rain help plants grow.

Animals find food
when new plants grow.
Animals that were sleeping
in winter wake up.
Many baby animals are born
in spring.

I Wonder . . . Animals go
through many changes in spring.
I wonder what other changes
happen in spring?

_____

_____

Circle the correct answer.

1. Which of the following
   words describe spring?

   (A) warmest season

   (B) long hours of sunshine

   (C) follows winter

S1E1c

17

2. Tell about summer.

_____

_____

_____

3. What are some ways you try to stay cool in summer?

_____

_____

_____

Summer

Summer is the season that follows spring. Summer is the warmest season of the year. People try to stay cool. They wear clothing that keeps them cool.

Plants grow in summer.
Young animals grow, too.
Young animals learn to find food.
This lamb eats a growing plant.

Compare and Contrast

How are spring and summer different?

Summary Spring and summer are times of warm weather and new life.

Tell about the weather in these seasons.

▶ **Compare and Contrast**
How are spring and summer different?

Spring	Summer

19

VOCABULARY

fall The season that follows summer. (*noun*)

winter The season that follows fall. (*noun*)

VOCABULARY ACTIVITY

Multiple-meaning Words

fall

Look at page 20. How is the word *fall* used on this page? What is another way you use the word *fall*?

S1E1c. Correlate weather data (temperature, precipitation, sky conditions, and weather events) to seasonal changes.

5 What Is Weather Like in Fall and Winter?

Fall is the season that follows summer.
It is cooler in fall.
People wear warmer clothes.
Leaves drop from some trees.

Animals get ready
for colder weather.
Some animals grow thick fur.
Other animals move
to places that have more food.
Many animals store food
for winter.

1. What do animals do to get ready for the cold weather?

_____

_____

_____

I Wonder . . . Some activities change with seasons. Tell two activities you do in fall and two you enjoy in winter.

_____

_____

_____

2. Circle words on pages 22 and 23 that tell about winter.

Winter

Winter is the season that follows fall.
It is the coldest season of the year.
Snow falls in some places.

Sometimes it is hard for animals to find food.
Some plants die.
Many trees lose their leaves.

3. Draw what a tree looks like in cold winter weather.

4. Circle the sentence that tells what happens to animals in winter.

Circle the correct answer.

5. Which words describe plants in winter?

Ⓐ Plants grow.

Ⓑ Plants die.

Ⓒ Plants sprout.

S1E1c

Summary Fall and winter bring cooler weather and slower growth.

Use your finger to trace arrows pointing to each season. Say each season as you touch the word. What shape did you trace?

_____

▶ **Sequence** What season comes before winter?

| winter |
| spring |
| summer |

The Pattern of Seasons

The seasons change in the same order every year.
The order is spring, summer, fall, and winter.

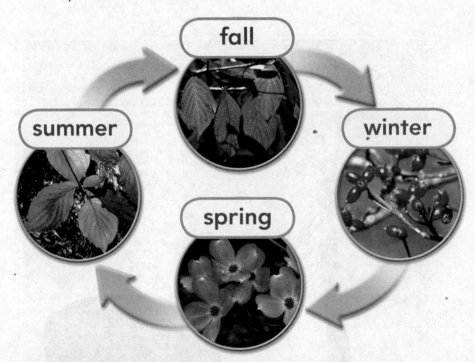

Sequence

What season comes before winter?

cloud Many drops of water together.

fall The season that follows summer. In fall, the weather gets cooler.

season A time of year that has its own kind of weather.

spring The season that follows winter. Many baby animals are born in spring.

summer The season that follows spring. Summer is the warmest season.

Choose three science words. Make up a story that uses your words. Tell a partner your story.

25

Visit www.eduplace.com to play puzzles and word games.

temperature How warm or cool something is. The temperature is cold when there is snow.

thermometer A tool that measures temperature.

water cycle Water moving from Earth to the sky and back again.

weather What the air outside is like.

winter The season that follows fall. Winter is the coldest season.

Responding

Think About What You Have Read

❶ **A tool that measures temperature is called a _____.**

   A. cloud

   B. summer

   C. thermometer

S1E1b

❷ What is a season?

❸ What can you tell by looking at clouds?

❹ How do you know it is windy if you cannot see the wind?

Chapter Review

K W L

WHAT DID YOU LEARN?

❶ Circle the correct answer on the page.

❷ A season is _____

_____

❸ You can _____

_____

❹ You know it is windy if _____

_____

27

KWL

What Do You Know?

Talk with a partner.

List what you know about weather
with water.

_____

_____

What weather do you see on
page 28?

_____

_____

Water and Weather

Contents

What Do You Want to Know?

Think about how water changes. What do you wonder about how water changes?

_____

_____

_____

_____

29

VOCABULARY

rain Water that falls in drops from clouds. *(noun)*

freeze To change from a liquid to a solid. *(verb)*

melt To change from a solid to a liquid. *(verb)*

VOCABULARY ACTIVITY

Use Pictures

rain

Use clues from the picture to help you understand what **rain** means.

GPS **S1E2a.** Recognize changes in water when it freezes (ice) and when it melts (water).

1 How Does Water Change?

Water is part of weather.

Rain is water.

Rain falls from clouds.

Rain is a liquid.

Rain is wet.

Rain is clear.

water

1. (Circle) the words that tell about rain.

2. Draw a picture of what you do in the rain. Write a sentence about your picture.

3. Circle the words that tell what happens when water gets very cold.

4. Draw an X on the ice on page 32. What season has weather cold enough to freeze water into ice?

GPS **CRCT Prep**

Circle the correct answer.

5. **The temperature turns very, very cold. The water in a pond will probably**

   Ⓐ change to ice.

   Ⓑ turn to liquid.

   Ⓒ become clouds.

S1E2a

32

Water Freezes

Water changes when it gets very cold. Water will freeze into ice when it gets very cold.

ice

To **freeze** is to change
from a liquid to a solid.
Ice is a solid.
Ice is cold and hard.

ice

6. Draw the glass shown on this
page. Next to it, draw the glass
shown on page 31.

Tell how they are alike and
different.

_____

_____

_____

7. Draw an X on the melted ice cubes. What made the ice cubes melt?

_____

I Wonder . . . I have something in a cup. The cup falls over. What was inside spills out. How can I tell if a solid or a liquid was in the cup?

_____

_____

_____

Ice Melts

Ice changes when it gets warm. Ice will melt when it gets warm. To **melt** is to change from a solid to a liquid.

ice

water

Water changes when the weather changes.
Water can change into ice when it is cold.
Ice can change into water when it is warm.

Compare

What is different about water and ice? What is the same?

Summary Water becomes ice when it freezes. Ice becomes water when it melts.

Fill in the blanks.

Temperature	Water
_____	frozen water
warm	_____

▶ **Compare** What is different about water and ice? What is the same?

Ice	Water
_____	_____
_____ water	liquid water

VOCABULARY

hail Round ice and hard snow. *(noun)*

sleet Frozen rain mixed with snow. *(noun)*

snow Ice that falls from clouds. Snow is white and soft. *(noun)*

VOCABULARY ACTIVITY

Use Words

snow

What words on page 36 help you understand what **snow** is? (Circle) them.

GPS **S1E2b.** Identify forms of precipitation such as rain, snow, sleet, and hailstones as either solid (ice) or liquid (water).

2 How Does Temperature Change Water?

Water in clouds will freeze when the air is cold. Different kinds of ice fall from clouds. **Snow** is ice that falls from clouds. Snow is white and soft.

snow

Sleet is another kind of ice that falls from clouds.
Sleet is frozen rain mixed with snow.
Sleet is wet.

sleet

1. List two kinds of ice that fall from the clouds when the weather is cold.

   a. _____

   b. _____

I Wonder . . . Sleet and snow are frozen ice that falls from clouds. What must happen before ice forms in clouds?

_____

_____

_____

2. Draw a circle around words that tell about hail.

CRCT Prep

Circle the correct answer.

3. The temperature is warm. There is a thunderstorm. The water that is falling from the sky is icy and hard. It falls as

Ⓐ snow.

Ⓑ sleet.

Ⓒ hail.

S1E2b

38

Ice in Warm Weather

Ice can fall from clouds when it is warm.

Hail is round ice and hard snow. Hail falls during thunderstorms. Hail can be small or big.

hail

High in the clouds
air can be cold.
Water in clouds can turn to ice.
Hail falls from clouds.

Classify

Is hail a solid or a liquid?

Summary Water can fall from the sky as a solid or a liquid.

Name the kinds of water that fall from the sky.

a. Solid: _____

_____

b. Liquid: _____

Classify Is hail a solid or a liquid?

Solid	Liquid
ice	water
_____	rain

39

Visit **www.eduplace.com/gascp** to play puzzles and word games.

freeze To change from a liquid to a solid. When water freezes, it changes to ice.

hail Round ice and hard snow.

melt To change from a solid to a liquid. When ice melts, it changes back to water.

Glossary

rain Water that falls in drops from clouds.

sleet Frozen rain mixed with snow.

snow Ice that falls from clouds. Snow is white and soft.

Draw rain falling from clouds, and show what a person wears when it rains.

Draw snow falling from clouds, and show what a person wears when it snows.

Chapter Review

What Did You Learn?

 CRCT Prep

❶ (Circle) the correct answer.

❷ Rain and snow are different

because _____

_____.

❸ Ice will melt _____

_____.

❹ It will _____

42 _____.

Responding

Think About What You Have Read

 CRCT Prep

❶ **To change from a solid to a liquid is to _____.**

A. freeze

B. melt

C. snow   S1E2a

❷ How are rain and snow different?

❸ When will ice melt?

❹ It is hot and cloudy. Will it rain or snow? Why?

What Do You Know?

Talk with a partner.

List what you know about light.

_____

_____

What does the light bulb give off?

_____

_____

Heat, Light, and Sound

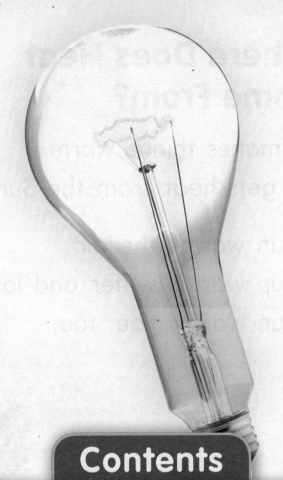

Contents

What Do You Want to Know?

Think about light.

Where have you seen light?

_____

_____

What do you wonder about light?

_____

_____

45

VOCABULARY

heat Something that makes things warm. *(noun)*

VOCABULARY ACTIVITY

Use Words

heat

Heat makes things **warm**. (Circle) the word **warm** on page 46. Draw an X on things the Sun warms.

1 Where Does Heat Come From?

Heat makes things warm.
Earth gets heat from the Sun.

The Sun warms the air.
The Sun warms water and land.
The Sun warms you, too.

Heat comes from other places.
A light bulb gives off heat.
Fire gives off heat.

1. Where does Earth get heat from?

_____

I Wonder . . . You are standing under a tree and you are cold. What could you do to get warm?

_____

_____

_____

_____

47

2. Tell how heat changes things.

Heat makes things _____

and _____ food. Heat

can also _____ things.

GPS CRCT Prep

Circle the correct answer.

3. A rock in a field begins to warm. What is warming the rock?

Ⓐ the Sun

Ⓑ the ground

Ⓒ the air

S1P1a

Heat Changes Things

Heat can make things change.

Heat makes ice melt.

Heat cooks food.

A fire gives off heat
when it burns.
You can feel the heat.
Heat can move things, too.
Look at the picture.
Heat from the flames
moves the air.
The air moves
the windmill.

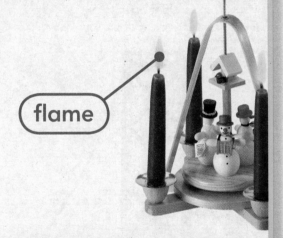

windmill

flame

Cause and Effect

What are some ways that heat causes change?

Summary   Heat makes things warm. The Sun heats Earth. Heat also makes things change.

Circle the things on page 49 that heat the air and make the windmill move.

Cause and Effect   What are some ways that heat causes change?

Cause	Effect
Heat	makes things _____
	makes things _____
	_____ food
	makes things _____

49

VOCABULARY

light Something that you can see. *(noun)*

shadow Something that forms when an object blocks light. *(noun)*

VOCABULARY ACTIVITY

Use Syllables

shadow

Break the word into syllables. Say each syllable aloud. Clap once for each syllable. How many syllables does the word **shadow** have?

S1P1a. Recognize sources of light.
S1P1b. Explain how shadows are made.

2 Where Does Light Come From?

Earth gets light from the Sun. You can see **light**.

Light comes from other places.
Fires give off light.
A light bulb gives off light.
They give off heat, too.

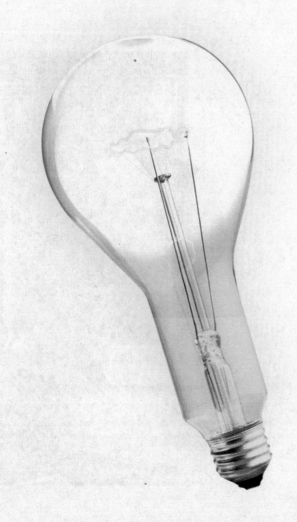

1. Where does Earth get light from?

_____

2. Circle the things that give off light.

3. Light passes through _____,

_____, and _____.

I Wonder . . . Plants need sunlight. Should you place a plant near a window or in a room with no windows?

_____

_____

_____

Light and Shadows

Light can pass through some things.
Light passes through clear glass.
Light passes through water and air.

Light does not pass
through some things.
Some things stop light.
Look at the picture.
No light passes through.

4. Change the picture on page 52
so that light does not pass
through the window.

Circle the correct answer.

5. Which of the following
stops light from passing
through?

Ⓐ wooden door

Ⓑ clear glass

Ⓒ air

S1P1b

53

5. Circle the shadow. Where would the Sun have to be to make this shadow? Add the Sun to the picture.

Other things stop some light from passing through. Sunglasses stop some light. Look at the picture. Some light passes through.

Your body blocks all light.
A dark shape called a **shadow**
forms when something
blocks light.

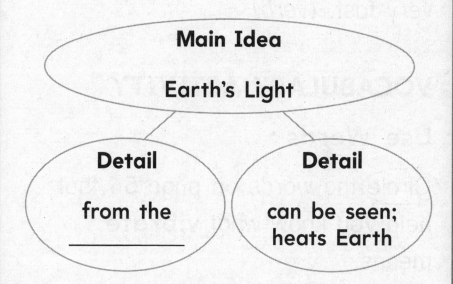

shadow

Main Idea

Where does Earth get its light?

Summary You can see light.

Circle the things on page 55 that make a shadow.

▶ **Main Idea** Where does Earth get its light?

```
          Main Idea

        Earth's Light


   Detail              Detail

  from the           can be seen;
  _____          heats Earth
```

VOCABULARY

sound Something that you can hear. *(noun)*

vibrate To move back and forth very fast. *(verb)*

VOCABULARY ACTIVITY

Use Words

(Circle) the words on page 56 that help you know what **vibrate** means.

3 How Is Sound Made?

You can hear **sound**.

Sound is made when something **vibrates**.

To vibrate means to move back and forth very fast.

Many kinds of things vibrate and make sound.

This frog makes sounds.

GPS **S1P1c.** Investigate how vibrations produce sound.

The space shuttle makes sound when it takes off.

1. Circle the pictures of things on pages 56 and 57 that make sounds.

I Wonder . . . Sound is made when something vibrates. How is sound made when two sticks are hit together?

_____

_____

_____

2. Draw a picture of something that makes sound.

3. Draw a picture of yourself. Make a sound. Draw an X on the place you could feel vibrations when you made the sound.

A bird makes sounds when it sings. You make sounds, too. Place your hand on the side of your neck. Now sing or talk. You can feel the parts in your neck vibrate.

Look at the picture.
These children are making sounds.
Sound can be music.

4. Use a red crayon to color the instruments that vibrate when you pluck the strings.

5. Use a green crayon to color the instruments that vibrate when you strike them.

6. Use a blue crayon to color the instruments that vibrate when you blow into them.

Summary You can hear sound.

Trace the vibrations from the drum to the boy's ear.

▶ **Draw Conclusions** How does the sound of a drum reach your ears?

> **Fact**
>
> A drum _____ when you hit it.

↓

> **Fact**
>
> The air around the drum _____.

↓

> **Fact**
>
> The air that vibrates makes parts inside your ear _____.

↓

> **Conclusion**
>
> You can hear the drum.

60

Hearing Sound

A drum vibrates when you hit it. The air around it vibrates, too. Air that vibrates makes parts inside your ear vibrate. Then you hear sound.

Draw Conclusions

How does the sound of a drum reach your ears?

4 How Are Sounds Different?

Not all sounds are the same.

Pitch

Pitch is how high or low a sound is.
Fast vibrations make a high pitch.
Slow vibrations make a low pitch.

high pitch

low pitch

VOCABULARY

pitch How high or low a sound is. (*noun*)

volume How loud or soft a sound is. (*noun*)

VOCABULARY ACTIVITY

Find All the Meanings

pitch

A word can have more than one meaning. You may know that the word **pitch** means "to throw a ball." The word **pitch** can also mean how high or low a sound is.

 S1P1d. Differentiate between various sounds in terms of (pitch) high or low and (volume) loud or soft.
S1P1e. Identify emergency sounds and sounds that help us stay safe.

61

1. When you yell, your voice has a

_____ volume.

I Wonder . . . A drum can make a loud sound or a soft sound. How can you change the volume of a drum?

_____

_____

_____

Volume

Volume is how loud or soft a sound is.
You make a soft sound when you whisper.
You use little energy to make a soft sound.

soft volume

You make a loud sound
when you yell.
You use a lot of energy
to make a loud sound.

loud volume

2. Circle the objects on page 63 that are being used to make a loud sound.

_____

3. Volume is how _____ or

_____ a sound is.

Circle the correct answer.

4. **When you use a lot of energy to make a sound, what do you hear?**

Ⓐ a soft sound

Ⓑ a loud sound

Ⓒ a low sound

S1P1d

63

5. What does it mean when a smoke alarm beeps?

_____

_____

6. Fire trucks make loud noises to warn you to get out of the way. Draw a picture of something that makes a sound that helps you stay safe.

Sounds Keep You Safe

Some sounds help to warn you.
These sounds keep you safe.
A smoke alarm beeps.
It warns you to go
to a safe place.

A fire truck makes a loud sound. It warns you to get out of the way.

Compare and Contrast

How is a high pitch different from a low pitch?

Summary Pitch is how high or low a sound is. Volume is how loud or soft a sound is.

Some sounds help to warn you. (Circle) the objects on pages 64 and 65 that make a sound that help keep you safe.

▶ **Compare and Contrast** How is a high pitch different from a low pitch?

Low Pitch	High Pitch
vibrates	vibrates
_____	_____

Choose one science word. Make up a riddle about this word. Tell the riddle to your partner. Can he or she guess the word?

heat Something that makes things warm.

light Something that you can see, such as light from a light bulb.

pitch How high or low a sound is. A violin has a high pitch.

shadow Something that forms when an object blocks light.

Glossary

sound Something that you can hear. Birds make sounds when they sing.

vibrate To move back and forth very fast. A drum vibrates when you strike it.

volume How loud or soft a sound is. A whisper has soft volume.

 Visit www.eduplace.com to play puzzles and word games.

Chapter Review

WHAT DID YOU LEARN?

❶ Circle the correct answer on the page.

❷ Three things that give off heat are

_____, _____, and

_____.

❸ Two things that make sounds that keep me safe are _____ and

_____.

❹ I can see a shadow when

_____.

Responding

Think About What You Have Read

❶ **Which tells how high or low a sound is?**

A. heat

B. light

C. pitch

S1P1c

❷ What are three things that give off heat?

❸ What are two things that make sounds to keep you safe?

❹ When will you see a shadow?

Magnets

KWL

What Do You Know?

Talk with a partner.

Draw an object made of metal.

Tell about the object.

Contents

What Do You Want to Know?

What do you wonder about a
magnetic field?

_____

_____

_____

_____

VOCABULARY

attract When objects pull toward each other. *(verb)*

magnet An object that attracts iron or steel objects. *(noun)*

magnetic An object that is attracted by a magnet. *(adjective)*

poles The places on a magnet where the forces are strongest. *(noun)*

repels When a magnet pushes an object away from itself. *(verb)*

1 What Are Magnets?

A **magnet** is an object that attracts some metal objects.
Attract means pull toward each other.
Magnets come in many shapes.
They come in many sizes.
They have many uses.

magnet

GPS **S1P2a.** Demonstrate how magnets attract and repel.
S1P2b. Identify common objects that are attracted to a magnet.

An object that attracts magnets is **magnetic**.
A metal called iron is magnetic.
A metal called steel is magnetic.
Most magnetic objects have iron or steel in them.

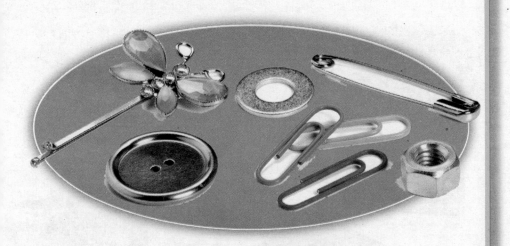

magnetic objects

1. List three objects in the picture that would be attracted by a magnet.

a. _____

b. _____

c. _____

Circle the correct answer.

2. Which is not attracted to a magnet?

Ⓐ iron

Ⓑ steel

Ⓒ plastic

S1P2b

3. On page 74, draw an X on each item that is not attracted to a magnet.

4. Fill in the blanks.

Objects

Not Attracted to Magnets	Attracted to Magnets
a. _____	a. _____
b. _____	b. _____
c. _____	

An object that does not attract magnets is not magnetic.
Glass and wood objects are not magnetic.
Neither are paper objects.
Metal objects that do not have iron or steel are not magnetic.
These objects do not attract magnets.

These objects are not magnetic.

Magnets Act on Each Other

Magnets have forces that act on other magnets.

The force can be a push.

It can be a pull.

Magnets have two poles.

The **poles** are where the forces are strongest.

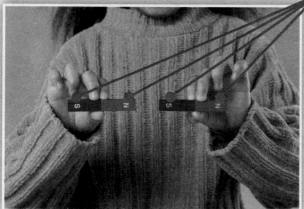

poles

5. Where are the forces strongest on a magnet?

_____

6. (Circle) the poles on each magnet.

I Wonder . . . How can you move a magnet without touching it?

_____

_____

_____

_____

7. Unlike poles _____ each other.

8. What will happen to these magnets? Why?

| S | N | | N | S |

_____

_____

_____

_____

Some magnets have letters on the poles.
N is for north pole.
S is for south pole.
Poles with the same letter are like poles.
Like poles repel each other.
Repel means to push away.
Poles with different letters are unlike poles.
Unlike poles attract.

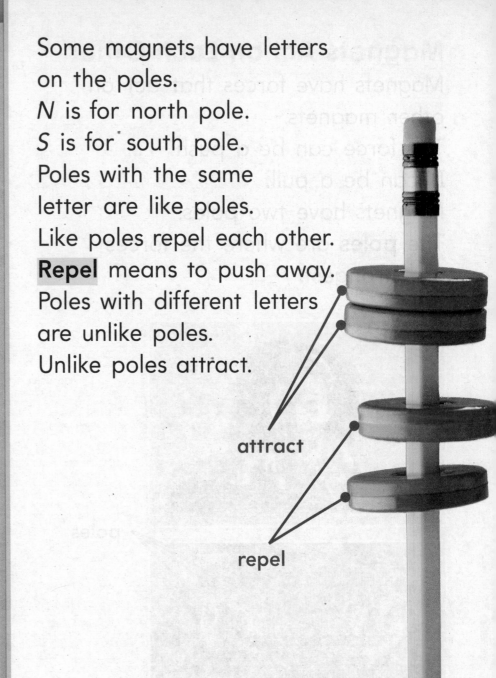

attract

repel

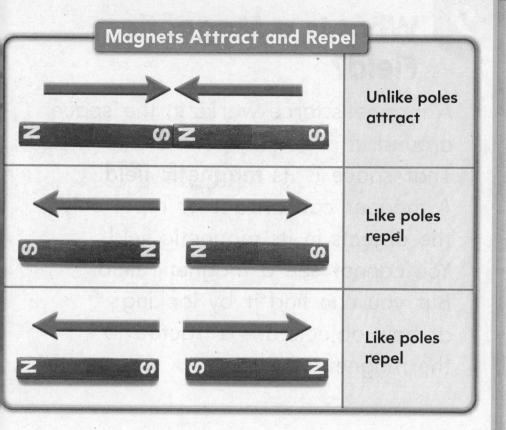

Magnets Attract and Repel

	Unlike poles attract
	Like poles repel
	Like poles repel

Cause and Effect

What happens when like poles are together?

Summary   A magnet is an object that attracts iron or steel objects.

Tell what magnets can do.

_____

_____

▶ **Cause and Effect**   What happens when like poles are together?

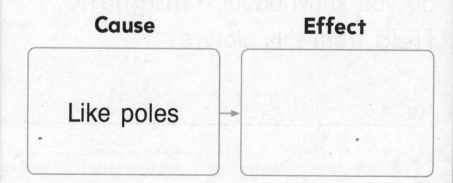

Cause	Effect
Like poles →	

VOCABULARY

magnetic field The space around a magnet where the magnet's force works. *(noun)*

VOCABULARY ACTIVITY

Use Pictures

magnetic field

Look at the picture on page 78. Circle the **magnetic field.** What do you know about a **magnetic field** from this picture?

_____

_____

GPS S1P2a. Demonstrate how magnets attract and repel.

2 What Is a Magnetic Field?

A magnet's force works in the space around it.
That space is its **magnetic field**.
A magnet can attract or repel only the objects in its magnetic field.
You cannot see a magnetic field.
But you can find it by looking at how objects are attracted to the magnet.

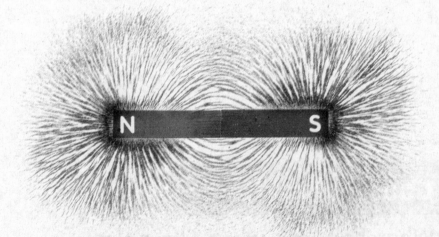

These are little pieces of iron. They are attracted to the magnet's poles. They show where the magnetic field is.

A magnet's force is strongest at its poles. The magnet does not need to touch objects to attract them. The force is so strong that a magnet can attract things without touching them!

Magnetic objects are pulled to the poles. That is where the force is strongest.

Compare and Contrast

How is the center of a magnet different from the poles?

Summary The space around a magnet where the magnet's force works is a magnetic field.

Where is a magnet weakest?

▶ **Compare and Contrast** How is the center of a magnet different from the poles?

Magnet	
Poles	**Center**
strong	_____

VOCABULARY

magnetic force The pushing or pulling force of a magnet. *(noun)*

VOCABULARY ACTIVITY

Use Words

Circle the words that describe a **magnetic force.**

S1P2c. Identify objects and materials (air, water, wood, paper, your hand, etc.) that do not block magnetic force.

3 How Strong Is a Magnet's Force?

The pushing or pulling force of a magnet is its **magnetic force**. Magnetic force can make an object move without touching it. Magnetic force acts on magnetic objects. It acts on other magnets, too.

These objects are pulled to the magnets by a magnetic force.

A magnet's force can attract objects through other things.
Objects can be attracted through paper and glass.
They can be attracted through plastic, water, and air, too.

Magnets work through pictures.

1. (Circle) the magnets on page 81.

2. A magnet's force can attract objects through other things. List five of these things.

a. _____

b. _____

c. _____

d. _____

e. _____

I Wonder . . . A magnet's force can attract things through other objects. I wonder what three things in the classroom a magnet's force can work through?

_____

_____

_____

Magnets work through air.

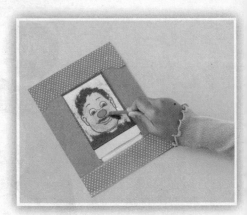

Magnets work through plastic.

Magnets work through glass and water.

Weakening a Magnet's Force

Magnetic force gets weaker as the object moves away from the magnet. A strong magnet can attract an object from far away. A weak magnet can only attract objects that are close.

Magnets work through paper.

3. Draw a magnet's force working through another object.

GPS

CRCT Prep

Circle the correct answer.

4. A magnetic force

　Ⓐ gets weaker when it is closer to an object.

　Ⓑ can move an object without touching it.

　Ⓒ can move a plastic object.

S1P2c

Summary Magnets can work from a distance.

In the top photo the magnetic force is _____.

▶ **Draw Conclusions** How can a magnet hold a picture to a refrigerator?

Fact
Magnetic force can work through _____.

↓

Fact
A magnet is _____ to the refrigerator.

↓

Conclusion

one piece of paper

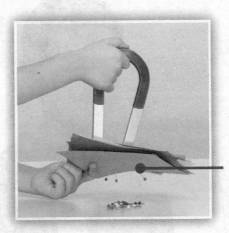

many pieces of paper

This magnet's force can pass through one piece of paper. It is too weak to pass through many pieces of paper.

Draw Conclusions

How can a magnet hold a picture to a refrigerator?

attract When objects pull toward each other.

magnet An object that attracts iron or steel objects.

magnetic An object that is attracted by a magnet.

magnetic field The space around a magnet where the magnet's force works.

Choose two science words. Write each word three times.

_____ _____ _____

_____ _____ _____

Work with a partner.
Test each other on the spelling.

Glossary

Visit www.eduplace.com/gascp to play puzzles and word games.

magnetic force The pushing or pulling force of a magnet.

poles The places on a magnet where the forces are strongest.

repels When a magnet pushes an object away from itself.

Responding

Think About What You Have Read

GPS CRCT Prep

❶ **The space around a magnet where the magnet's force works is its _____.**

   A. poles
   B. magnetic force
   C. magnetic field

S1P2c

❷ How should you hold two magnets so they pull toward each other?

❸ Where on a magnet is the force strongest?

❹ Predict what will happen if you put a magnet near a pile of steel paper clips.

Chapter Review

What Did You Learn?

GPS CRCT Prep

❶ Circle the correct answer.

❷ Magnets will pull toward each other

if their _____ poles are

_____.

❸ A magnet is strongest at

_____.

❹ The paper clips will be _____ toward the magnet because

_____ are magnetic.

87

Plants

KWL

What Do You Want to Know?

Talk with a partner.

List what you know about plants.

_____

_____

What plants do you see here?

_____

_____

Contents

What Do You Want to Know?
Think about what you need to live.
What might a plant need?

_____

_____

What do you wonder about plants?

_____

_____

VOCABULARY

sunlight Light from the Sun.
(noun)

VOCABULARY ACTIVITY

Break It Apart

sunlight

Write the two smaller words that make up this word.

_____ + _____

GPS **S1L1a.** Identify the basic needs of a plant. 1. Air; 2. Water; 3. Light; 4. Nutrients.

1 What Are the Needs of Plants?

Plants need air.

Plants need light.

Plants get light from the Sun.

Light from the Sun is called **sunlight**.

sunlight

Plants need water.

Some plants need a lot of water.

Some plants need a little water.

1. Circle the plants being watered on page 91.

How are these plants getting the water they need?

_____

CRCT Prep

Circle the correct answer.

3. Plants need air, light, and

Ⓐ water.

Ⓑ clouds.

Ⓒ a flower pot.

S1L1a

Summary Plants need air, water, light, and space to grow.

Draw a picture of a healthy plant.

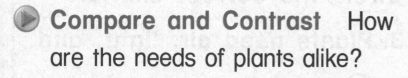

▶ **Compare and Contrast** How are the needs of plants alike?

Small plants need	Big plants need
_____	_____

92

Space to Grow

Plants need room to grow.

Room to grow is called space.

Big plants need a lot of space.

Small plants need a little space.

Compare and Contrast

How are the needs of plants alike?

What Are the Parts of Plants?

Plants have parts.
The parts help plants do
many things.

VOCABULARY

flower The part of a plant that makes seeds. *(noun)*

leaves Parts of a plant that make food for the plant. *(noun)*

roots Parts of a plant that take in water and hold the plant in the ground. *(noun)*

stem The part of a plant that connects the roots to the other plant parts and holds up the plant. *(noun)*

S1L1c. Identify the parts of a plant—root, stem, leaves, and flower.

1. (Circle) the name of each plant part.

GPS CRCT Prep

(Circle) the correct answer.

2. **Plants have roots, stems, and**

Ⓐ food

Ⓑ water

Ⓒ leaves

S1L1a

Plants have roots.
Plants have stems.
Plants have leaves.
Some plants have flowers.

leaves

flower

stem

roots

Parts of Plants

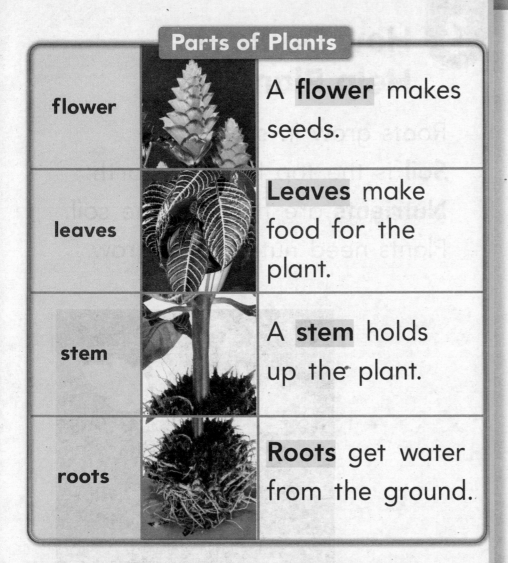

flower	A **flower** makes seeds.
leaves	**Leaves** make food for the plant.
stem	A **stem** holds up the plant.
roots	**Roots** get water from the ground.

Classify

Which part of the plant makes food?

Summary Plants have parts that help them get what they need to live.

Which plant part gets water from the ground? _____

▶ **Classify** Which part of the plant makes food?

Parts of Plants

makes seeds	make food	holds up the plant	get water

95

VOCABULARY

nutrients Materials in the soil that plants need to grow. *(noun)*

soil The loose top layer of Earth. *(noun)*

VOCABULARY ACTIVITY

nutrients

Circle the words on page 96 that help you know what **nutrients** mean.

3 How Do Roots Help Plants?

Roots grow in soil.
Soil is the top layer of Earth.
Nutrients are things in the soil.
Plants need nutrients to grow.

soil ———

roots ———

  S1L1c. Identify the parts of a plant—root, stem, leaves, and flower.

Roots take in water.

Roots take in nutrients.

Roots help hold up a plant.

roots

1. Circle the part of the plant that takes in water and nutrients from soil.

GPS CRCT Prep

Circle the correct answer.

2. _____ take in water and nutrients and help hold up a plant.

Ⓐ leaves

Ⓑ roots

Ⓒ stems

S1L1c

Summary Roots of a plant take in water and nutrients from soil.

Some roots are good to eat. What are some roots that people eat?

_____

▶ **Main Idea** How do roots help a plant?

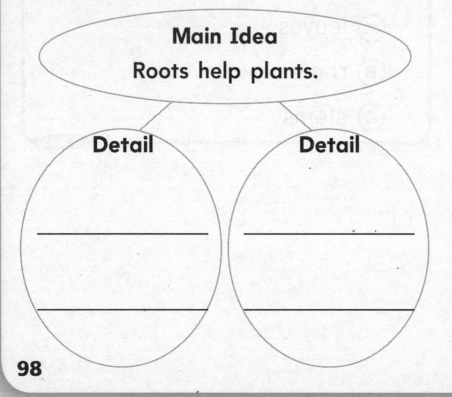

Main Idea
Roots help plants.

Detail

Detail

98

Different Kinds of Roots

People eat some roots.

Carrots and beets are roots.

People eat carrots and beets.

Main Idea

How do roots help a plant?

How Do Leaves Help Plants?

Plants need sunlight to live and grow.

VOCABULARY PREVIEW

sunlight Light from the Sun. *(noun)*

VOCABULARY ACTIVITY

sunlight

Circle the word **sunlight** on page 99. Where does **sunlight** come from?

_____

S1L1a. Identify the basic needs of a plant. 1. Air; 2. Water; 3. Light; 4. Nutrients.

99

I Wonder . . . I know that plants need light. How would the plant on the left look if it got more light?

_____

_____

_____

Change the picture to show how the plant would look.

All plants need light. Plants need light to grow. Plants will not grow well if they do not get the light they need. The plant on the left did not get light.

How Leaves Work

Leaves take in sunlight.

Leaves take in air.

Leaves make food for the plant.

The plant uses the food to grow.

1. List why plants need leaves.

_____

_____

_____

GPS **CRCT Prep**

Circle the correct answer.

2. Plant _____ take in sunlight and air and make food.

Ⓐ leaves

Ⓑ roots

Ⓒ stems

S1L1a

Summary Leaves take in sunlight and air to make food for the plant.

Tell about the different kinds of leaves.

_____

_____

▶ **Cause and Effect** What do leaves do for plants?

Cause	Effect
_____	_____
_____	_____

Different Kinds of Leaves

Leaves can be big.

Leaves can be small.

Leaves can be flat.

Leaves can have points.

leaves

Cause and Effect

What do leaves do for a plant?

flower The part of a plant that makes seeds.

leaves Parts of a plant that make food for the plant.

Draw the parts of a plant that take in sunlight to make food.

Draw lines to match the words with the same meaning.

nutrients   dirt

soil   food

Glossary

nutrients Materials in the soil that plants need to grow. A plant takes in nutrients through its roots.

roots Parts of a plant that take in water and hold the plant in the ground.

Glossary

soil The loose top layer of Earth.

stem The part of a plant that connects the roots to the other plant parts and holds up the plant.

sunlight Light from the Sun.

 Visit www.eduplace.com to play puzzles and word games.

Chapter Review

WHAT DID YOU LEARN?

 **CRCT Prep**

❶ (Circle) the correct answer.

❷ A plant needs _____

_____

❸ Leaves help plants _____

_____

❹ People can _____

_____

106

Responding

Think About What You Have Read

 **CRCT Prep**

❶ **Things in the soil that help plants grow are _____.**

A. sunlight

B. nutrients

C. stems

S1L1a

❷ What does a plant need to live?

❸ How do leaves help plants?

❹ How can people help plants get what they need?

Animals

 KWL

What Do You Know?

Draw an animal you know.

Name each of its body parts.

Contents

What Do You Want to Know?
What do you wonder about animals?

_____

_____

_____

VOCABULARY

shelter A safe place for animals to live. *(noun)*

VOCABULARY ACTIVITY

Use Pictures

shelter

Look at the **shelter** on page 111. A picture helps you know the meaning of the word. What do you know about this **shelter** from the picture?

S1L1b. Identify the basic needs of an animal. 1. Air; 2. Water; 3. Food; 4. Shelter

1 What Are the Needs of Animals?

Animals need food.
Some animals eat plants.
Some animals eat other animals.

Shelter

Some animals need a shelter.
A **shelter** is a safe place for animals to live.
A nest is a shelter.

nest

1. Draw a shelter that a bird uses:

CRCT Prep

Circle the correct answer.

2. What is a safe place for animals to live?

Ⓐ water

Ⓑ shelter

Ⓒ land

S1L1b

111

3. Many animals use their

_____ to _____ in air.

I Wonder . . . The picture on page 112 shows a fish. How does a fish get the air it needs?

_____

_____

Animals Need Air and Water

Animals need air.
Some animals use a nose to get air.
Fish use gills to get air.

nose

gill

All animals need water.
Animals get water by drinking.

Draw Conclusions

How are all animals alike?

Summary Circle the things animals need to live.

pillow   water   food   air

Draw Conclusions How are animals alike?

Fact
Animals need _____.

↓

Fact
Animals need _____.

↓

Fact
Animals need _____.

↓

Conclusion
All animals _____.

VOCABULARY

fins The body parts a fish uses to move in water. *(noun)*

wings The body parts a bird uses to fly through the air. *(noun)*

VOCABULARY ACTIVITY

Use What's After

fins, **wings**

The ending –s has been added to these words. The ending means "more than one." Tell what each word means.

  S1L1d. Compare and describe various animals—appearance, motion, growth, basic needs.

2 What Are the Parts of Animals?

Animals have body parts.
The parts help animals find food.
The parts help animals stay safe.

bush baby

ears

eyes

legs

Using Body Parts to Stay Safe

quills

stinger

claws

smell

sound

color and shape

1. Circle the body parts of each animal that help it stay safe.

2. Write the name of the animal under each picture.

CRCT Prep

Circle the correct answer.

3. **What do animals use to stay safe and find food?**

Ⓐ body parts

Ⓑ fresh air

Ⓒ food

S1L1d

115

4. A  uses _____ and

_____ to move in water.

5. A uses _____ to fly through the air.

I Wonder . . . Why does a lion have such strong legs?

_____

_____

_____

Parts for Moving

Body parts help animals move.

A fish uses a tail to move.

A fish uses **fins** to move, too.

fin   tail

Some animals walk.
They use legs to walk.
Some animals fly.
They use **wings** to fly.

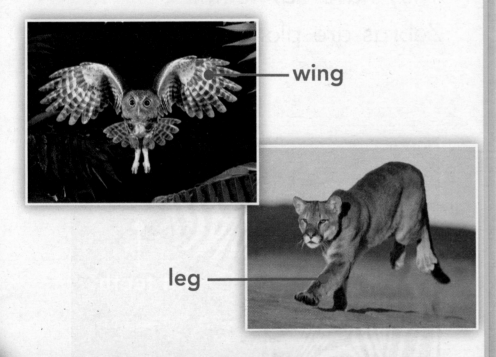

wing

leg

Main Idea

Why do many animals have legs?

Summary

Name the body parts that animals use to help them live.

_____

_____

_____

▶ **Main Idea** Why do many animals have legs?

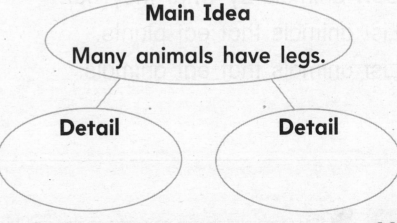

Main Idea
Many animals have legs.

Detail

Detail

VOCABULARY

plant eater An animal that eats mostly plants. *(noun)*

meat eater An animal that eats other animals. *(noun)*

VOCABULARY ACTIVITY

Classify Words

plant eater, **meat eater**

Sort animals by what they eat.
List animals that eat plants.
List animals that eat animals.

GPS **S1L1d.** Compare and describe various animals—appearance, motion, growth, basic needs.

3 How Do Animals Use Their Mouths?

Some animals eat plants.
They are **plant eaters**.
They have flat teeth.
Zebras are plant eaters.

flat teeth

Some animals eat other animals.
They are **meat eaters**.
They have sharp teeth.
Lions are meat eaters.

sharp teeth

1. Draw food that a zebra eats.

2. Draw food that a lion eats.

 **CRCT Prep**

Circle the correct answer.

3. **What body parts do animals NOT use to eat?**

Ⓐ legs

Ⓑ teeth

Ⓒ ears

S1L1d

4. Draw a bear's teeth.

I Wonder . . . Dogs have sharp teeth. What kind of food can dogs eat?

_____

Some animals eat plants and animals.

They have flat teeth.

They have sharp teeth, too.

Bears eat plants and animals.

They have flat teeth and sharp teeth.

Other Mouth Parts

Some animals do not have teeth.
They have other parts.
The parts help them eat.
This animal uses its long tongue
to get food.

| zebra | lion | chameleon |

5. This animal uses its flat teeth to

grind plants. _____

6. This animal uses its sharp teeth

to tear meat. _____

7. This animal uses its long tongue

to catch food. _____

121

Summary   Animals use their mouths to eat. What kind of teeth do plant eaters have?

_____

What kind of teeth do meat eaters have?

_____

▶ **Compare and Contrast**

How are a lion's teeth different from a zebra's teeth?

Lion's Teeth	Zebra's Teeth

122

Birds have beaks.
A beak helps a bird eat.

beak

Compare and Contrast

How are a lion's teeth different from a zebra's teeth?

fins The body parts a fish uses to move in water.

fin

meat eater An animal that eats other animals. A meat eater has sharp teeth.

plant eater An animal that eats mostly plants. A plant eater has flat teeth.

Pick two science words. Write each word three times.

_____ _____ _____

_____ _____ _____

Work with a partner.
Test each other on the spelling of your science words.

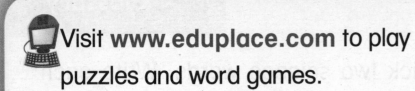
Visit **www.eduplace.com** to play puzzles and word games.

shelter A safe place for animals to live.

shelter

wings The body parts a bird uses to fly through the air.

wing

124

Responding

Think About What You Have Read

❶ A safe place for animals to live is _____.

A. fins

B. wings

C. shelter

S1L1b

❷ Why does a fish have fins?

❸ What do animals need to live?

❹ Why isn't a bicycle an animal?

KWL

What Did You Learn?

❶ (Circle) the correct answer.

❷ A fish has fins to _____

_____.

❸ Animals need _____

_____.

❹ A bicycle is not an animal because

_____.

125